Bearings

Bearings

Isobel Dixon

Nine
Arches
Press

Bearings
Isobel Dixon

ISBN: 978-1-911027-02-7

Cover artwork © Lynne Stuart
www.ideainaforest.org

First published April 2016 by:

Nine Arches Press
PO Box 6269
Rugby
CV21 9NL
United Kingdom

www.ninearchespress.com

Printed in Britain by:
The Russell Press Ltd.

For my fellow travellers

Contents

Finsong

Alphabet of breath
and fish and fowl,
words the gills and wings
of the world we love and suffer in.

Kingdom of mackerel skies,
the cloud's anatomy,
glottal branches of sense,
beautiful trachea, click-locking vertebrae.

We husband our resources,
tend. O tender emperor,
your cheer a mute command,
more subjects than you dream unwind

the bandages. The curling scrolls,
inscrutable cells. The dorsal fin
of fortune flicks, scales flex.
Mutable, curious, entire,

unfurl in the flux,
the deep, beyond-breath alphabet.

i.m. James Harvey

Messenger

Russet and frost
roadside fox
surprised
to be sidelined so fast.

Stop press
on the early news
he was delivering
tip-toeing across tar –

Abuja, Tripoli,
Hurricane Irene,
and the sky's
new supernova –

Now his ankles
are delicately crossed
but he's sidelong
on the grass.

Mercurial reversal,
the still-fine feathers
of his bushy tail
ruffled by wind

but his grin's
the giveaway,
a Janus mask.
His ear is snicked,

a young buck's mark.
He is beautiful.
Whose job is it to bury
a dead fox? you ask.

Dream Song for John Berryman

She sets her wineglass delicately down
and Henry harrumphs inwardly
at all the world's geometry and fission nuclear
in thát. Then smitten, smarting
from her wide indifference, he spills
his own. Hubbub and salted tables

and the stain admonishes all night. A map,
lost territory. Will they, reproachful hosts,
invite him back, or shoulder coldly to the C-list?
Calmati, Henry!
O, Mr Bones I knows the score.
Henry must tame the lust-quest –

knees, whiskey phantasies, the conscience
unappeasable. Wreckt, wracked, there hover
over Henry hummingbirds, flown in
from gentler climes. Henry slo-mos their wings,
the flexing tints. And sips. But can Henry write it?
Reader, he díd, and was desired.

"A Part of Me is Gone"

It's not just twins, identical,
who feel this way
(thinking as one),
same-egged, conjoined,
deep life-long linked
till hit and run –

or old age in my case:
not twinned, but fathered,
equally bereft.
Death, it seems, the fiercest
raider of identity,
for the survivor too – self's theft.

Once genetic double,
mutual-celled;
equalled, answered, met –
you were almost only goodness,
I'm the damaged bit that's left.

Pinball Electra

You and your robot bride, I scoff
(the sport of waking her, waking her),
cold metal clattering to fleshen
out the supine girl, evince
that throaty laugh's ideal
appreciation of your skill.

You ribbed me back –
how I, Electra-like, keep
harping on my theme.
And I dream a dark arcade,
where the pinball king
has made a game of genius,

to make him breathe, if
I play it right. Shake the cabinet
with the volleys, flippers
to defibrillate the dormant heart,
a silver hail on whitened skull.
Make him turn and see.

No cheat codes for this level,
a hall of earnest girls play on.
Coinfall after coinfall,
the expectation of that crucial voice,
shattering the case's glass.
Make him speak to me.

In Which I Am Urged to Let Myself Go

There'll be time enough, elsewhere, to fret
at how the indelicate prosper.
Let's drink to the whimsy of the jolly-boat,
the evening cavalcade.
You find me garrulous? Then speak.
Even a cuckoo has more tongue.
Quid pro quo. Quid pro quo. Quid pro quo.

In Which Things Go Too Far

The lawn has not been mown in weeks.
It lays there moaning to itself, only I
can hear the rhizomes' thin green whine.
Everything has a voice
if you pause to listen. Why else do we stop
our ears: phones, buds, muff, cuff, boxed
about the lobes. *Wheesht.* Won't you just *shut up*.

In Which We Pack It In and Shut Up Shop

Nothing turns out as you plan; don't
give me your Easter Island stare.
Mice and men and the praying mantis,
equal prey. And I am tired
of the pelican mother sideshow here.
Get a life. Find a lift, hitch a ride. Stick out
your thumb. Fuck off till the cows and kingdom come.

In Which Dogs Feature Only Metaphorically, Alas

It's easy enough to break the habit of a lifetime:
I'll have what you're having.
My years of simple living chucked out of the window,
gone to the dogs – Borzoi,
Labradoodle, poodle, lap. And the Lapis Lazuli Girls
are in the wings. I'm hoping one will show me
how she does that thing, like Cleopatra, with the kohl.

Treasure

I was lazied by the sun, doused in my slick of shade.
You were water-babying about, as usual,
quickened, easy in your new saltwater skin.
I woke with a start to see the sun moved on,
and you still in the cooling sea. I could spot you
bob and dive, bob up and dive again: almost comical,
a touch of music hall, my anxious, snorkelling seal.
Not chasing fish – the ring I'd slipped onto your finger
months before slid from your suncreamed hand
and spiralled slowly to the Red Sea's floor.

A tantalising zigzag – you almost caught it
twisting down, but the current and the light aslant
had tricked you, grasping water, sifting sand,
till at last you had to meet me on the beach, downcast,
say the sea had beaten you, admit that it was lost.

Who couldn't love you for your efforts at recovery,
how time and time again you dived and tried
to keep me from this news. That night, we drank to truths
beyond our trinkets; found a silver makeshift
that's become the very thing. And since you helped me
conquer fears of drowning, know the water, breathe,
I have dreamed of salvage: how with easy buoyancy,
past skeins of gilded fish, we'd fin the mutual depths,
find betrothal gold submerged with Pharaoh's chariots.

For Jan

Dubai Creek, Ramadan

We haven't fasted, but have eaten iftar fish, cooked Asian-style,
"as you prefer", marvelling at boori, barracuda, shark,
dorade, laid out on ice, a sameways-facing glass-eyed fleet.

But now, outside, the air's as hot and thick as soup.
My glasses mist up when I step out of the air conditioning's
grip, and beyond the parking lot, the four-by-fours

(one equipped with extra jerrycan and spade for sand),
we see the men, stripped, shining, to the waist, unload
the cardboard cartons to the quay. *Peak Performance, Adidas,*

a sporting wharf. They are barefoot, and their daytime clothes hang
spread out on the decks' carved balustrades, in the hope of drying
in the night's humidity. Further on, work done, men look up

from their huddles – I imagine cards but don't know enough
and don't dare to stare or photograph. But they stare back,
challenging and curious: few tourists walk this heat, this late.

Outside the boatmens' mosque, the congregated bicycles,
each one festooned: the ornamental everyday of plastic bags,
more damp draped cloth. A tall man stoops out from the light, lays

his wrung-out kurta carefully on the box-clipped hedge that skirts
a flitch of lawn. There will be a garment harvest here at dawn.
A line of trucks wait for the morning load, reliable Toyotas,

regulation white, but on the flatbed railings, metal cutwork,
simple filigree – heart, diamond, butterfly – hand-fashioned
blazoning and cadency. There's a sudden whiff of za'atar

and a dhow lies heavy in the water, heaped with fat stitched
sacks. The herb is overwhelmed by cinnamon, a heady war
of spice. Above the blue-and-white balconies tethered

to the quay, gargantuan ranks: the gleaming towers – pinnacles
of sheer design, dune-mastery – breathe their expensive chill.

The Town Hall Passion

My sisters took me home
before the crucifixion:
old enough to see the miracles,
the Massacre of the Innocents
in Technicolor, but not the bloody end.
But what of the resurrection
I was also spared,
the reassuring glory of the Risen Lord?

Transfixed, resisting, more
than a little dazed by hours
of sunlit pageantry –
the projector's murmur,
reel-change clattering –
our sitting room furniture
had a different sheen to me,
the floorboards redolent

of wax and frankincense.
And our neighbours, dressed up
in their town hall best –
mayor, hairdresser, priest,
the lady from the hardware store,
the man who ran the cinema –
sat on, white host, beneath
the ceiling's plaster cumulus.

How dark the oxblood polish
of the fireplace shone.
The banisters hummed.

I held on to the newel post,
resolved – dear life, O Love! – resolved.

Seville Yellow

I have a case of Gothic Cathedral Neck,
my head tipped back to gawp and snap
at arches, colonnades, mosaics,
                              Evangelistic Animals.

At the tomb of Cristóbal Colón, his bearer's shoes
are burnished to a reverend bronze.
The skewered pomegranate too –
                              good travelling luck?

His bones criss-crossed the sea, restless reliquary,
as fingers here stroked prayers to carry loved ones
safely home, still warm, like those eighteen,
                              Magellan's lucky men.

Perhaps that's some descendant now, polishing,
painstakingly, the altar's silver blossoming. Does he love
or hate his daily chore? – buffing ludicrous
                              curlicues, religious glitz.

I much prefer the modest potter saints, Justa y Rufina,
Goya's girls in mustard sashes, radiant pallor, eyes transfixed.
I'd like a tawny lion to lick my toes like that
                              (but wouldn't want to die for it).

A mechanical mantis – alien convert – cranes its Day-Glo
neck to pray, or probe, the fabulous altar-piece's flaws.
I pause to gaze at the trompe l'oeil screen
                              hiding this scrutiny, repair,

but I'm heading for the broader vistas the Giralda's
ramps and stairs afford. If it weren't for the bells
this could be Marrakech, the mosque, Jemaa el-Fna Square.
                              A pinch of Moorish history.

Over the rooftops' gardens, pools, the ochre walls,
Calatrava's bridge lifts up its bright white angel's wing, a harp –
but the angle's like the jutting trotter of the poor jamon
                              pinioned in every little tapas bar.

¡Ay! – The gargoyle gutters grimace back. Below,
the bored nags stamp and twitch their living rumps
at flies and tourists lured to take a turn in carriages
                              with bright segmented wheels

which echo winter fruits just warming from the green
in avenues of scented trees. The peach-faced lovebirds
flit from Isabella's flying boat into the palms
                              and I sip my pale dry fino

to my Spanish-Irish friend, her charms: her golden hair,
dimpled serenity, the bearing of a painted Virgin,
Saint or Queen; her breathy, chuckling sense
                              of all that's wondrous and absurd.

For Roísín

In Which I Am Given a Very Wide Berth

Not quite the Madwoman in the Attic (just give
me time), up here in my eyrie,
penning my memoirs in lemon juice (if you turn up
the heat, all will be clear),
I'm practising to be The Invisible Wife.
The best sort of woman, you might say. A deep
vocation, one of the subtlest arts. A job for life.

In Which It's All a Jolly Fine Mess

just like the time you left the Risk™ out in the rain
and all of Europe turned to mush.
I never liked that game, the glint you got
at *Lebensraum*, I'd rather be the Scottie
going to jail. And I've served my time.
Professor Plum's a dismal footnote now;
that sorry slogging pawn will never make the crown.

In Which You Feel the Scorch of Industry

Can you feel the draught in here? It chills the spine
to think of all the little seamstresses,
that fire. A river of cloth, beware
the spark. Humming at Singers,
busy little treadle feet & O sewing sisters, mark
that twist of smoke!
They have locked the doors to keep you safe at work.

In Which the Amazon Does Not Appear

How far the drifting berg is from the wadi,
never the twain, yet give it time.
Track the furrows of my brow back
to the dongas of my youth.
Ford the drift, die in the sloot. Explorers once,
we're washed-up duffers
on this pinchbeck island now, another calving coast.

The Cock-Eyed Southern Cross

*'Charles will not admire the Southern Cross because he says that
it is cock-eye. I cannot see that this constitutes an indictment.'*
– Reginald Rankin, *A Subaltern's Letters to His Wife* (1901)

There's as much chance
of an interstellar spring clean,
tidy reckoning of stars,

as there is that earthly powers-
that-be will cease to turn
their kingdoms upside-down

sending men to distant wars.

Late Knowledge

I have forgotten the Periodic Table of the Elements,
apart from the famous few
and the look of the waxy scroll of text
unfurled against the science lab's wall,
Earth's Ten Commandments graphed in code.
I went with my father in the night as a little girl,
when he was setting up experiments,
sat long and studied it, in fascinated ignorance.

And I have forgotten basic chemistry,
apart from the dancing fizz of phosphorus
and the day my father's sulphurous show-and-tell
expelled him and the Standard Nines, out
to the quad in search of air. The same quad where
I watched the senior girls rehearse their witchiness
around mysterious brew – their fire burn
and cauldron bubble scorched into my brain.

Goniwe, like my father, taught, not far away,
but then I didn't know his name; Cradock
just another dusty settlement, minor satellite
to our own, all unrest pressed out to the margins –
his Lingelihle, our Umasizakhe stirring up
a history not taught in my calm classrooms.
And he was sent to prison in the town
where I was born, the Communist suppressed

and then so inconveniently returned.
I have forgotten, if I ever read,
what the *Eastern Province Herald* said
about their disappearances – Sparrow Mkhonto,
Fort Calata, Sicelo Mhlauli, Matthew Goniwe,
the Cradock Four. If they printed anything at all
until their permanent removal from society
(that terrible permission from on high) was clear.

Who thought to bring the telephone wire?
(Strangled, stabbed and shot – so dangerous
one killing wasn't death enough?)
Who poured the petrol on each face
to sear away the individual flesh?
What did they talk of while the bodies burned?
And which one cut off Matthew's hands?
What calculation was this and what settled score?

In the lab, my father readied for his class;
I watched Lady Macbeth try to erase the marks.
But I drive now with those men, Olifantshoek
to Bluewater Bay – the threatening
and the defiant, frightened for their lives.
That road, the darkest pass. These are the nights
we've no will to recall, but must, how
something evil always in among us was.

In memory of Matthew Goniwe, Sparrow Mkhonto,
Fort Calata & Sicelo Mhlauli

The Other Cheek

1. Uncle Peter

The chainsaw leaped to kiss him
like a long-lost friend, too fierce and fond,
and drew a new mouth where none was before.

I think of the shock, how he held the flap
of his face – a tender cut – till the flesh was stitched,
a cartoon criss-cross on his rough sandpaper rasp.

The scrape of that morning peck, obligatory,
and all the gruff hellos and long goodbyes,
car stuffed with pumpkins, cabbage, and a leg of mutton,

carefully wrapped in layers of the bloody news.
Yesterday's boycotts for tomorrow's beef;
a nation's mayhem, our provincial life.

2. Mark

How old Ruff snapped: warming his creaking hip
in a patch of sunlight, woken from his dreaming
of the flock by a thick-tongued whippersnapper boy

with trusting Chinese eyes. Hapless cousin,
plucking at his jaw, peering in the wolf-mouth,
past the warning growl, till the sudden lunge

to teach the pup respect. The pain, surprise,
Mark's piercing wail, his punctured cheek.
That smile through blood and tears, our big Down's boy,

trying to hug the tail-down dog, waving goodbye
as he ducked into the car, reassuring us: 'Don't worry,
Uncle Peter, don't be cross with Ruff, I'll be OK. Don't fuss.'

3. *Elgin – A Brown Study*

Granny's garden always was Elgin's domain:
saffron canna lilies, shaggy chrysanthemums,
beds of roses, a honeysuckle fence. His borders

neater than the carved and recarved map,
Mpuma Koloni, our scraps of the Cape.
His sunny terraces a welcome escape

from the gloomy sitting room: he went about
his work never minding my games,
stopping to show, with a wave of his pipe,

a frog, a giant snail, and once, from beneath
a plant pot, coiled and brown, a snake.
As brown as his dusty overalls, but the scales

a-shimmer with a boot-shine gloss. He'd shine yours
that way too, if you asked, a line of shoes
all buffed-up on the kitchen porch at dawn.

I remember the wedding on Mount Pleasant,
old cine-film ceremonial: his suit and dignity,
Angelina's borrowed hat and gloves.

How he'd gently cluck the hens back in at night.
But mostly, just a tall and quiet man, brown overalls,
brown hands, holding a spade, a watering can,

a pipe. The pipe that seemed a part of him,
its polished wood an echo of his skin.
Those shreds he pinched out, nutty-sweet,

from the orange plastic Boxer pouch. And
the long slow punch of nicotine that later ate
away his mouth, his smooth brown cheek.

4. *Bhekinkosi & the Boerboels*

Turn your face away. Flinch, retch, at the thought
of the trusted gardener come to the house at night,
bringing back the keys. And the dogs who knew
his smell and face by day, trust him not.
Their instinct says: *Tear him apart.* They try.

This is where you stop your ears. No one
should hear, or more, endure such viciousness.
But think, if you can, how a man survives
his mangling, some days in despair, sick
to the very marrow now of hospitals.

How the children flee. But what we guard,
our boundaried life, makes monsters of us all.
Turn the savaged cheek, not only for the work

of grace – accept the surge of horror, and the heart's
wide-open tear. Pray, rage, for the comfort of the hurt,
amends, repair. For no repeating of a savage history.

Pickings

A man pushes his rubbish
juggernaut up 7th Avenue,
Melville. Cresting the rise,
then swiftly switching sides
to brake – his shoulders braced –
his junk ship's following wind,
that swift acceleration down the hill,
a slope of now-dishevelled affluence.

His mate, in Fair Isle pullover
(a find?) careens around the corner,
laden even more, merging
their flotsam fleets.
They've got in well before
the garbage trucks, cracking
the bins like jacaranda pods,
shucking them clean.

I imagine the whole Heath Robinson
embarrassment of cast-off riches:
Nelson's fractured spyglass;
Napoleon's tattered glove;
the battered Homburg
of a fallen president; a sleek jet
fashioned in an emptied flask
of Johnnie Walker Blue;

and all the debris that's more
usually jettisoned.
Spring efflorescence trumpets
noisy fuchsia; giant hibiscus
clamours loudly for attention,
too. A blur of sweet Bohemia.
Petal, rubble, scrap metal –
a supernova waits to blow.

Above, three mousebirds
delicately decorate the wires,
views unperturbed: Forget the barbs,
alarms, the locks, breakers
of locks, the pocket pickers,
trashbound whistlers,
raasbekke, karweiders
of the loot, these streets are ours.

Trade Matters

copal coconuts beeswax ambergris
ivory rhinoceros horn cowrie shell

(also known as blackamoor's teeth)
always be sure to check the teeth

for a slave to snore in sleeping
is counted a very great fault indeed

make them run a little way
there should be no defect of the feet

a child worth a pound or two
in Zanzibar will fetch twenty in Persia

no one buys an adult slave (domestic –
wild from inland is a different matter)

their masters never part with them
till they are found incorrigible

but the wild slaves though saleable
are a source of lawlessness and robbery

the worst is the treacherous weather
the tedium, the wearisome monotony

every merchant hopes to leave
as soon as he can realise a tidy sum

every agent would persuade
his employer to recall him

Women at a Christmas Party, Robben Island, 19th Century

The one in charge stands firmly at the table's head
against the panelled door. Her bosom is a prow, the buttons fixed
between a constellation of pale polka dots, upon a bodice
of some black and shiny cloth. Her festive hat's a neat confection
perched above the scraped-back bun, her forehead smooth
    and bare.
Your probing gaze could make hers stern, or sad.

Two children sit among the women, hard to see at first:
low at the table, one half hidden by the other, shy.
The scene's familiar, yet off-kilter; you're not sure
why it should so unsettle you. The table's laid, sliced breads
    and meat.
The smooth unlabelled bottles' curves give off a shine –
from the black-and-white, you glean that old dark green.

Slim vase and white chrysanthemum: a petalled comet
to encircling moons, the cloth-draped heads. A strange
miscellany – two dark Voortrekker women, kappies starched
to high parabolas, steep arches guarding them, as if
against the Highveld sun. Caught in the camera's flare
one's cheek is pitched in shade, her mouth a blur.

The other turns her crumpled face, to stare skew-eyed,
this story's dwarf: light teases out the surfaces, carbuncular,
in clear relief. One's toppled teacup headdress hovers,
alien, at Polka Dot's right hand. Another's turban
has the tribal elegance of the Sudan. The simpler
shawls or veils could mark Islam, but this is Christmas –

if you turn the page, the caption tells. One wears, anomalous,
dark glasses tipped down on her nose; below,
her mouth is wide and sensuous. Lace-collared,
one blunt face looks out, direct; around her shoulder, wary,
her companion peers. The big-looped metal tankards wait,
none raised – the lepers' hands kept in their laps.

It is hard to tell what is the camera's shake, how the subjects
stirred, or your heart's own flinch, from the bulge and smudge
and ruin of shadow captured here. Above, lopped
parts of flags hang limply down. From below, you trace
a silvered streak – at first perhaps a streamer, tinsel,
but it's just the paper's flaw, a tear, a crease.

Truths & Reconciliations

Pragmatic whitewash,
rainbow complacencies,
the miracles forgot –
but would you forgive the man
who made your father blind?
No single hand put out those eyes,
no blade or burning brand –
but you knew there was an Island,
though you never thought
of the detail at the time:
the slow and bitter years,
the chipped-out days,
the worn-down line of men
bent in the burning sun
to the glitter of the lime.

In Which It Will Go Heavily With You

Nobody gets away with it, nobody ever gets away.
A too-long summer, such indulgence,
means the winter's harsh. Everybody knows
you have to see the fiddler right.
The Economy of Seasons, the Doctrine of Clouds.
This blighted continent, our bruiséd globe –
O shelter us. Close your eyes, my friends, and count, and count.

In Which the Air Misleads

It would be wonderful, she said. A would-be
windfall's what I heard.
A susurration in my ears, breeze shushing
in the leaves. How the wind it runs
you ragged, winds you up and wears
you down. A fortune, eardrums,
speakers blown. *Pffff*. Been, done, and oh-so-woebegone.

In Which the Organ Speaketh Well

The Cathedral's fine acoustics are a boon, just don't
whisper what you don't want told
to all the gathered flock at scones and tea.
We're all seeking consonance, forgiveness, mastery.
And take *that* how you want to,
either way. You get your followers, your leaders –
which are you? Pull out the stops – *Clarion! Diapason!* – and see.

In Which the Heavenly Lights Descend

The moon by any other tune will call the tides –
karmic obol, cosmic nickelodeon.
But the rose window's blown and the shards
remaining cast a stain upon
your cheek, a florid mark. Is that a daisy
or a dandelion, and is it time again?
The moon sprawls in a ditch, regards the drunkard's thistledom.

DARK MATTERS

Reading Cosmology on the Cherry Hinton Bus in Spring

Pinkshift, whiteshift.
The Big Bud,
the Magnolia Way.
These trees are island galaxies.

Spring has come late this year,
like what I've learned.
And how to balance this burgeoning,
the oscillating green,
with the dark behind, before.
Our imprecision, what we cannot grasp,
or weigh.

The blackbird doesn't care
for measurement:
a tug, a gulp, a yellow blink.
A wormhole with no worm,
a punctuated lawn.

Homing

Sent far afield, where they cannot spoil
the clarity of the experiment,
the pigeons fly home from Whippany,
back home to the horn listening in to the hiss:
electrons rattling, the echoing universe.

They know their way, they have the beak for it,
while we flounder in the strip-lit shopping malls,
the grey parkades. Someone's lost
because her mind's on deeper matters
than the change for the machine –

she's almost cracked The Great Equation;
while my mind's on metaphors, and tea.
Cold load's the laundry left all morning in the drum
and saving the appearances is what I do
each morning with a touch of base and gloss.

Humdrum. *Ho-hum.* We know our impreciseness,
judge our loss, and carry on. And carry on.

Materiality

makeshift   shipshape   deepspace
        early scary dreams
roughsmooth   blackwhite
shapeshift   swellshrink
           mineshaft
           brainshift
       silken silent scream

Dark Matter
does the dark matter
        O, the dark mutters
        Dark Mother
        a darker moth
      the darkling mote –

me-grained
megrimmed
        a mute has-been

Learning

I want to touch the screen
       of death between us –
a tap of QWERTY   Morse
telepathy
and tell you
         in some mirror universe's fireside
chair
of what I'm reading now

       the missing-matter mystery
       dunkle Materie

I want to see your eyebrows knit
       that cogitating pause
and hear your 'That's interesting, because…'
The enlivening flow of thoughts
you've stored
as if somehow
       just for this moment
         and my eager listening ears.

Presentiment

The shadow on the lawn –
out of the corner of your eye,
see it grow.
Feel the evening cool advance,
the slow summoning of dew.

Deep in the throat of the dark,
the growl,
the low vibrato cogwork of your fear,
ratcheting up. Wound-up,
wounded, wounding –

shrink back from the spirit's dusk.
The child, crossing the grass
in sunlight,
passes the shadow-bar.
The twilight girl carries its ashen cross.

Why?

Because I say so.
The world isn't fair.
Do as I say, not as I do.
Handsome is as handsome does.
Manners maketh the man.
Beggars can't be choosers.
If wishes were horses,
beggars would ride.
The poor will always be with us.
God in His wisdom knows.
Lambda (at present unknown).
Lambda, at present unknown.

Economy Cosmology

'Matter tells space how to curve. Space tells matter how to move.' – John Archibald Wheeler

What tells the jasmine's starry carpet
how to spread and spill,
a fragrant wave, over Departures and Arrivals
at Aeroporto Galileo Galilei,
a sweet profusion greeting us
before the cosh of Ryanair's cut-price blues
and Stansted's colder steel and glass.

You and your spheres, Eudoxus,
consider this, the oscillating universe.
Consider us, consider us.
Galileo Galilei, Sidereus Nuncius,
starry messengers, O Copernicus.
In all this flurry, fuss and flux,
I pause and rest my temple
on the toughened porthole glass,
think of motion, heavens, maths.
The pulsing stars, the ticking
Wall Street screens,
my high perspective
on a world I cannot grasp.

In Which the Traveller Despairs of Art

The Sphinx is crumbling in my hands.
Tutankhamun's visage shrinks.
O Egypt, how could you build the pyramids
and sell such tat, even that which isn't yours to trade:
the elephants, the carved giraffes,
from so far south. *The Russians, they like*
the animals. He finger-pops a rifle shot, and grins.

In Which I Understand the Seedpod and the Rock

You have the knack of disappearance
from within, growing still
as is your wont, so when it all evaporates
and you can finally drift away,
the taste, the thirst, are all forgot.
What's long-cherished is a husk;
the closest to you ever are stone last to realise.

In Which the Trees Agree

All the times you knew, before you'd got to *five*
that they were gone, the big kids,
and the joke of hide-and-seek was being *all alone.*
But the jacaranda was your friend.
The mulberry understood. The cypress sighed
its melancholy at the cruel world,
the pity, bones and feathers of your shoebox-buried birds.

In Which, as Henry Knew, the Books Are Cooked

My Other, You and I, we are foredoomed.
Our trampling empires wade
through the debris, the whole carcinogenic
wheeze of Life. Jaded,
radioactive, the First & Last Worlds
clasp each other, bosom enemies.
For you, special price, my friend – we're stewed.

Jerusalem Stone

The British Mandate's
good aesthetic sense
made use of other stone
a grave offence
and so the Holy City
glows in honey tones –
except the grey blade
slicing through the butter shades:
the wall they call a fence.

The Occupation

You come here to Jerusalem, for books?
What business took you then, on to Nablus?

No business. Just a friend.
A friend. She glances back to her dark screen:

I and its words are weighed. *Are you carrying anything*
for anyone? That officious tone. *Have you any gifts?*

My bags have gained a brightly coloured dot,
some primary code. My belly twists

despite the contents' innocence – powdery,
dark-green za'atar, soap in milk-white blocks.

No. (No? What friend, proud of their land,
does not give gifts?) She waves me on.

And then the same quick question, asked again, again,
by taxi drivers, checkpoint soldiers, concierge –

perhaps the notebook had them on their guard?
No, no, I am not a journalist.

I am *not* a journalist.
The small word *poet* does not pass my lips.

dead siege

these dead sea salts soothe the skin:
                                                but not the heart
the ventricles falter as you soak in
all the news
                        uneasy pump
                                        na-blus, ga-za, & ra-ma-lah

and all the ziggurats of creamy soap
                stacked in a warehouse without industry
can't wash
                        can't wash away

they too would float
                                        like blocky bodies
        on the minerals

                        pale convoy
                                flotilla of olive oil
                                        a sea of soap

a million melting mesas bumping up
                                                whitening the map

the wind whips salt into your face
                                encrusted armoury
                        ludicrous to think you could defy the law
of gravity
                the siege embankments   attack ramps   drones
                                ma-   sa-   da-
the twisty garrisons of history

                the old men sleep in their shattered olive groves

Gaza

Cease/Fire – count the cost.
One truth is, death is always
disproportionate.

Nouns

Roads, Walls

Walls, Roads

Roads, Walls, Flags
Martyrs, Walls, Checkpoints, Flags
Prisoners, Walls, Martyrs, Orphans
Orphans, Widows, Prisoners, Walls

Checkpoints, Walls, Checkpoints

Walls, Shells

Shells, Sons, Walls
Sons, Funerals, Coffins, Flags
Sons

Songs, Sons, Funerals, Shells
Shells, Walls

Talks, Walls, Missiles, Drones
Mortars, Missiles, Drones, Shells
Drones, Airstrikes, Talks, Ceasefire

Airstrikes
Ceasetalks

Airstrikes, Missiles, Drones

Drones, Bulldozers, Tanks

Tanks, Bulldozers

Ceasefire

Talks

Spare Us

Spare us the pride of facts on the ground,
the obstacle we can't get round.
The immovable But.
Give them a finger,
we've eaten the hand.
The unhealable wound.

Where on Earth

There is an East Bank
of the heart, across the river,
in the direction of the dawn,
where the young men play fierce football,
comb their hair carefully for girls,
seek to defeat their desperate rivals –
their enemies only in sport and love.

In Which We Scat, Tra-La, the Last Vibrato Of A Single String

We walk through the hum of the summer
young on the Spanish Steps, seemingly
unscathed, on our way to another night
of all that jazz. The rose sellers grow
darker by the day and the roses more –
unreal. Upstairs, the microphone's aimed
at the bass's waist, her nifty clef.

In Which the Walls are Closing In

The room is hot, the prosecco cheap. But
you're a bad jazz club clapper (yeh)
(the wrong offbeat)
and the trompe l'oeil library
wallpaper won't rescue us now.
Shirrrrr, says the percussionist, *shirrr tik-tik,*
Shirrrrr, a-dikadikdik-aaaaa, to a dying fall.

In Which You (Too) Could Give a Hoot

Another day, another fugue. Isadora dances
only fleetingly on film. The myth intact.
Not every princess feels the pea.
This very randomness is why it is so precious
and so easy to lose track. You bet.
Innittowinit. Towittowoo. *Whoo.* Who – ?
Wisdom's not the same as photographic memory.

In Which, More Jazz

You can drown in the black lakes of piano lids.
I know. Grand Rapids, down in one.
Dying Falls, Niagara-style, a barrel of laughs until
it's your turn, luv. *Ooo.* Who knew?
You thought, like age, it only happened to the careless
ones. You'll still be working on that riff, the great improv,
when push, my daring darling, comes to shove.

Deliver Him

On the black road of the treadmill,
blocking out my breathing
and the tinny techno-loop with Handel,
but eyes fixed on the TV:

my feet falter at the news, the scrolling ticker tape.
Birthday candles, his small face. *O Messiah –*
zoom in, a tight green focus, forest far
from desert canvas, foreign wars.

The volunteers fan out, red, orange lozenges
in aerial shot. A field, a fallen tree.
He could have been the subject of a criminal act.
He could have left of his own volition.
André, Andrej, Andrew. Scotland. Three.

Beyond the Fragile Geometry

The jewelled arch, the glass's stain,
the light of the nave that filters past
the solitary figure in the pew.

A toppled glass, the shattered pane,
the rising water in the grass.
Children at play after the rain

on Sunday afternoon. The fire's crackle
in the grate. A little girl in scarlet
mackintosh beside the lake.

The shattered glass, the spreading stain.
The lone confessor disappears,
the running figure on the grass

calls out too late: the ice is cracked,
all's already lost and known.
The axon flares, the shiver

of presentiment; a city's bridges,
twisted synapses. The mind's mosaic,
what's past fragmented, fitted

with what's seen aslant – through a glass
darkly, milky eyes, a murky veil.
A drill screams shrill into a wall

and the shark's jaws, the skull's gape,
have no more force and fear than this,
grief's beastly roar, a father's twisted face.

Japan Notebook, December 2004

1. *Hiroshima Morning*

Crossing a river,
washed with winter sun, we head
for the museum.

Okinawa G.I.s
on a day-pass follow us,
cropped heads like schoolboys

bent over displays –
the glass-cased explanations
of technologies

and strategy, the blunt
statistics of great bitterness.
This calm Boxing Day,

the sound of water
flowing over stone. A liquid
balm for memory.

2. *Museum at Noon*

Urged by the archive's sign –
"Look Up the Perished People" –
urgently, I read.

Morning feigning peace –
bright August day, but before
the sunset, ruin.

The dry-tongued dying
try to shed their burning skins.
The river swallows them.

Bodies float and bump
like rafts; boy soldiers hook them
to the littered banks.

The blood-red rubble
smoulders; hidden cells begin
slow motion simmering.

A woman's melted
spectacles. A child's flayed cheek.
The mosquito net

become cascades of flame.
A school's charred wall chalked
with the missing's names.

3. Lunch at the Mall

Stunned, silent, at the tram,
we read of how they fixed
the line – just days.

A youthful steel band
at the shopping mall – a girl
jumps at her xylophone

in pure delight. I
cannot hold the camera still,
shake at the brightness

of the instruments,
sunlight on steel, hot island
tunes, the leaping girl

a living flame. Recall
the words of a photographer:
the shutter pressed in hell.

4. Osaka Afternoon

"Ambitious Japan":
The bullet train conveys us
east, at speed. We sleep,

uneasy in our skins.
In Osaka's aquarium
we spiral down

the ocean temple,
stare at swimming wonders
of the Pacific Rim.

We are suspended
too. Not in our element.
Circle as restless

as the whale shark
in his tank, dreaming of fault
lines, as the rays glide,

shadowing. I am
dried and skeletal, my soul
a ghostly spider crab.

5. *Kyoto Night*

Our neat ryokan
room with sushi, sake,
samurai TV,

another hara-kiri
scene. The news in Japanese:
a ripped rice-paper

world, a splintering.
The word for *harbour wave.*
The news sinks in.

I read the *Fire*
and Earthquake Safety Info
closely, yet again,

and feel the past
and future tremors
of our origami lives.

Ikizukuri
活き造り

Be careful what you wish for. Especially when out of your depth.
Jet-lagged, hungry, bamboozled by the flight, a new world

steeped in ceremony. The Daily Special's cheap,
seems clear, among the bristling kanji. You have to choose.

You have to eat. The splash and thwack-thwack-thwack,
the smooth delivery, sashimi ornament. Now you know it's fresh,

swimming, beautifully skewered, towards the west:
a crenellated fish, still twitching on the plate.

You can see its little gills, their dry-air flap. Every scale
and fractured fin sending out fading alarms. We're all critters

of habit, to the last. But pick up your chopsticks. Bite.
Ignore the lagging nerves, their lies. This flesh is already dead.

Spew

Lasso, lasso, lasso
the sprinklers sough.
For coolth, you can lean
into the wet sheet sails
draped on the line
already drying
in the whipcrack afternoon.

Becalmed, your breath
the only stir
in the supine night,
you can line your spine up
with the wall's sheer white,
let the plaster take
your body's heat.

Flip the pillows
on the griddle of the bed
seeking out the only
sweet spot left
to lay your head.
Hold the milk jug
from the fridge against

your cheek, brief chill.
But your pooled
blood simmers on –
you will be spat out
for its lukewarm spill
and the heart's dull pull:
ba-dum, ba-dum, ba-dum.

In Which I, As Befits a Lady, Glow

You're almost a third character in my plot.
I wish you weren't.
The way the heat becomes the villain of the piece;
the way you rage and *sweat*.
The landscape looms, the city steals the scene.
Upstaged, I Exit Left,
Pursuing Bear. Come back anon to hear what happens next.

In Which Bad Dancers Hold No Sway

It's you again, I see, back here already for the easy dance.
Segue, sashay my way,
before the bloom is off the peach. Champagne
and goulash, schönen
Blauen Danau, *blahdiblah*. Sekt and Violins 'R' Us.
Also sprach The Űber-Girl:
The Devil take the waltz. Give me the rippling coda every time.

In Which, the Switch

And yes, the credits roll, but you don't get a mention,
though you watched right to the bitter end,
in case. It was ever thus. So much fuss, for so little
of all of this. No crumb of comfort
for the understudy, not unless Herself does really break
a leg. Deus Ex Machina, have Mercy on Us.
Oh, the lilies are sublime. Your note was sweet, their scent divine.

In Which a Flower is a Loaded Gun

Sir, you have a smear of pollen on your sleeve –
let me brush it gently off
before it settles, stains. Perilous, these blooms
despite their whiteness, all it takes
is just one brush against those saffron spears –
But I digress, forget myself. Your room is ready, yes.
The Aga Khan was once a guest. The rainfall shower's new.

Doppelgänger

*I have been doomed to such a dreadful shipwreck: that man
is not truly one, but truly two.*

Alter Ego
     I   –   You   –   I
                                     Doppelgänger
                 darling
                         dreaded
        self   self
                 inscape of selves

                    •• ••

Each mortal thing does one thing and the same:
. . myself it speaks and spells,
Crying Whát I dó is me: for that I came.

And yet, did you ever remark that door?
It was a fine dry night; frost in the air;
the streets as clean as a ballroom floor.
Small sounds carried far –
and out of the night
the doubled man, damned Juggernaut.

"If he be Mr. Hyde," he had thought,
"I shall be Mr. Seek."

Seek, seek and ye shall find
so profound a double-dealer,
a profound duplicity of me:
these polar twins
both sides in deadly earnest.

..   ..

lizard meniscus
Herzog's albino crocodile
        surfaces
                    peers mutant moon-eyed
                    at its pale
divided self
suspended in a viscous slick of history
                    double-visaged
visionary   spies viciousness, ancient and modern

My little saurian
        what do you make of the mess we're in?

..   ..

How long do you mean to be content?
the man on the terrace asks the poet, marked to drown.
Not long, not long, Zoroaster mutters
to himself from the verdant shrubbery,
where Herzog's Doppelgänger crocs will run amok
among the topiary, one day,
ere Babylon is dust.

..   ..

71

secret sharer
shore leave sailor shrinks
from his face on the shoulders
of the beaming butcher bloodied
at his screaming saw
beef brisket pierced by snagtoothed sun
a disc of gleaming stainless steel
gives back their
mutual face

.. ..

she
wears her hearts
on her sleeve
both marked for the waltz
her curvaceous self
and this elusive sylph
dissolve the flesh self
self same   same self
watch
sshh

.. ..

umlaut
vowel bending
coupled nought
double walker
Doppelgänger
truth will out
what have you brought?

.. ..

In Which Fine Feathers Fetter Us (I)

It's manners maketh the man, in a manner
of speaking, and how you evangelised
thát one, all the opened doors, the coat-sleeves
eased. But this is not a puddle,
sir, it's an abyss, your chivalry's just a civil way
to flog a long-dead horse. Let me – Let *me*
take that. You've no idea, this purse, its weight.

In Which Fine Feathers Fetter Us (II)

Your charm grows wearisome, the way
you measure your effects, as if
each girl's a tuning fork so you can strike
the better note, some later date.
We parry, counter-pose. I recognise your expertise,
the cut of your jib, how this is rigged.
But, oh the line of your wrist, the world in the fold of a cuff.

In Which I Learn to Hold the Pose

First, the blossoming lotus, now we're willows
in the wind. A little creaky
in this breezy twilight, and I sense your focus
isn't what it was. The phantom
of her fair young coconut flesh, and sweet –
O Scorpion! Down Dog!
I'm in a half-bind here. Stop blocking my drishti.

In Which, the Gram that Crackt the Globe

Online check-in quakes the stay-home soul,
fell weight of The Journey
To Be Undertook. The whole sweaty endeavour,
to-and-fro, and what on earth for?
Your pitch-black footprint stylised, Hang Ten,
Yin-Yang, tattooed & filtered snap-
and-share, offset by a foreign chambermaid's hefty tip.

Ellon

What are we to do with all this sky?
Swifts swoop and stitch it
to the glistening grass,

bring flighty news of clouds
that gather   pass   disperse
as birds do,

chirruping the breeze.

Here even the breeze
has water in.
The grass is fat with juice,

the river laps your skin.

The cloudlight turns,
pale stone. The turbines
make their stately signs –

alien druid presences
absorbing winds
into their whiteness,

making fire.

The wide earth's washed
in several silences.
The grass tufts nod.

This day
will be like another day
and not.

Holyrood

Here on the slopes
of Arthur's Seat
I lie down with the crows.
Let the grass speak.
Let the cool grass heal
my broken feet.

High up on the Crags,
someone has rolled away
the painted stones
and what they spelled.
But the crows know
what they said.
'Yes!' they caw, and 'yes!' again,
around my dreaming head.

Always Leave Them Wanting More

Impossible news.
I bought you a drink just the other day
passed it casually into your hand
through the crush – it was almost time –
grinned over my shoulder,
turned back to the bar.

Mustn't stay out too late,
you said with your glittering, puckish look
and slipped away.

i.m. Michael Donaghy

Wake

Looking back in the boat
as the island recedes
to the engine's growl,
how the double stream cleaves,
divides and cleaves,
how we leave
a white road on the sea
for a while.

Notes

'Late Knowledge' – previously published as 'Setting Up Experiments'. 'The Cradock Four'(Fort Calata, Sicelo Mhlauli, Sparrow Mkhonto and Matthew Goniwe) were killed by the South African Security Police in the Eastern Cape in 1985.

'Pickings' – Afrikaans: *raasbekke* – loudmouths; *karweiders* – carriers, porters.

'Trade Matters' – draws on some lines from *The White Nile* by Alan Moorehead (Hamish Hamilton, 1960), as well as original writings on Zanzibar and slavery by explorer Richard Burton in 1856 and by Captain Thomas Smee of the British research ship *Ternate*, which visited Zanzibar in 1811.

'Women at a Christmas Party, Robben Island, 19th Century' – inspired by a photograph in *The Island: A History of Robben Island, 1488-1990*, edited by Harriet Deacon (David Philip Publishers and Mayibuye Books, 1996).

The 'Dark Matters' sequence was written for the premiere of composer Roberto Rusconi's *De Materia Nigra et Obscura* performed by Klangforum Wien for 'Music in the Space Time Continuum' at Kings Place, June 2013. Richard Panek's *The 4-Percent Universe: Dark Matter, Dark Energy and the Race to Discover the Rest of Reality* (Oneworld, 2011) is the source of the John Archibald Wheeler epigraph and was a compelling and enlightening pleasure during the writing of this sequence.

'Beyond the Fragile Geometry' – inspired by Nicholas Roeg's film (based on Daphne du Maurier's short story) *Don't Look Now*, especially the film's memorable opening scenes.

'Doppelgänger' – written as part of a project with composer Roberto Rusconi for the premiere of his *De Imago (Materia) Sonora*, taking inspiration from Schubert's *Der Doppelgänger*, and performed by the Kairos Quartett at Kings Place in April 2013. The opening epigraph and some subsequent lines are from Robert Louis Stevenson's *Doctor Jekyll and Mr Hyde*. The sequence also draws on lines from the poem 'As Kingfishers Catch Fire' by Gerard Manley Hopkins and Percy Bysshe Shelley's verse drama *Prometheus Unbound* (from Act I: *'Ere Babylon was dust, / The Magus Zoroaster, my dead child, / Met his own image walking in the garden. / That apparition, sole of men, he saw.'*) Mary Shelley said a month before his death her husband reported that in a dream he had met a figure of himself walking on the terrace who asked, "How long do you mean to be content?" (*The Letters of Mary Wollstonecraft Shelley*, edited by Betty T. Bennett, Johns Hopkins University Press, 1980). And the haunting albino 'crocodiles' (actually, they're alligators) from Werner Herzog's film *Cave of Forgotten Dreams* sidled their way into the poem as well.

Acknowledgements

Several of these poems have been published or recorded before and I would like to thank my fellow artists and the editors of various publications for the encouragement and collaboration. These publications include: *Berryman's Fate* (Arlen House, 2014, edited by Philip Coleman), *Coin Opera II* (Sidekick Books, 2013, edited by Kirsten Irving and Jon Stone), *The Island Review* (edited by Malachy Tallack), *Magma 58* (edited by Laurie Smith, with Richard Morris), *Magma 59* (edited by Roberta James and Alex Pryce), *Poems in Which* (edited by Nia Davies and Amy Key), *Poetry Salzburg Review* (edited by Wolfgang Görtschacher and Andreas Schachermayr), *Prairie Schooner* (edited by Kwame Dawes), *Slow Things* (The Emma Press, 2015, edited by Rachel Piercey and Emma Wright), *Writers' Hub* (edited by Rebecca Rouillard).

'Treasure' was written and performed for Roddy Lumsden's 28 Project, the Four Quartets night in 2011. 'Dubai Creek, Ramadan' was shortlisted for the Strokestown Poetry Prize 2012, judged by Thomas McCarthy and Mary O'Malley. 'Late Knowledge' was originally published on Birkbeck's *Writers' Hub* and recorded for the Poetry Archive as 'Setting Up Experiments'. 'Truths & Reconciliations' was written and filmed for Mandela Day at the British Museum on 18 July 2010. *The Island Review* hosted the later film of the poem, directed by Jack Wake-Walker of Algorithm Films in April 2014. 'The Other Cheek' was shortlisted for the Live Canon Prize 2014, judged by Glyn Maxwell and published in the prize anthology. 'Spew' was published in English and Dutch translation on *Vertaallab* edited by Rozalie Hirs. Several poems were recorded for the Poetry Archive in 2015 and can be heard on their site.

The 'Dark Matters' sequence was written for the premiere of composer Roberto Rusconi's *De Materia Nigra et Obscura*, performed by Klangforum Wien for 'Music in the Space Time Continuum' at Kings Place in June 2013. 'Doppelgänger' was also written as part of a project with Roberto Rusconi for the premiere of his new work *De Imago (Materia) Sonora*, performed at Kings Place in London by the Kairos Quartett and EXPERIMENTALSTUDIO des SWR, Freiburg. Jack Wake-Walker made a short film of the poem, *Döppelganger*, without Rusconi's music, which was shown at the premiere in April 2013.

My thanks to the editors of all of these publications, the competition judges and all those involved in ZAPP (The Southern African Poetry Project) and the Poetry Archive, especially Georgie Horrell, Morag Styles, Richard Carrington, Anne Rosenfeld and Oli Hazzard. I am indebted to the wonderful Jane Commane of Nine Arches for her clear eye, care and good cheer during the making of this book. Admiration and appreciation to my inspiring creative collaborators Simon Barraclough, Luke Heeley, Chris McCabe, Liane Strauss, Christopher Reid, Róisín Tierney, Doug Robertson, Roberto Rusconi and Jack Wake-Walker.

And with the deepest love and gratitude to Jan for the ongoing journey.

~